ANNE FLEMING

Pedlar Press | St. John's NL

For information, write Pedlar Press at
113 Bond Street, St John's NL A1C 1T6 Canada

cover art Jacob de Gheyn (II), 1575 — 1625
(details from) *Vier studies van een kikker*
courtesy of the Rijksmuseum, Amsterdam

illustration dead bird & bike: Anne Fleming; pattern
(spine & inside covers): Beth Oberholtzer

design Oberholtzer Design Inc., St John's NL

typeface Archer

printed in Canada Coach House Printing, Toronto ON

LIBRARY AND ARCHIVES CANADA CATALOGUING IN PUBLICATION

Fleming, Anne, 1964-, author
Poemw / Anne Fleming.

Poems.

ISBN 978-1-897141-76-2 (paperback)
i. Title.

PS8561.L44P63 2016   C811'.54   C2015-906393-0

ACKNOWLEDGEMENTS
The publisher wishes to thank the Canada Council for the Arts and the NL Publishers Assistance Program for their generous support of our publishing program.

 Canada Council Conseil des arts
for the Arts du Canada

 Newfoundland Labrador

poemw

ANNE FLEMING

for Cindy

dead & alive

autobiography

Questions for Isabelle Gunn

academia.edu

dead & alive

Why The World Would Be Better Off Without People

What I want to say about pigeons,
these bottom-heavy vs teetering in the wind

these lugs wobbling down a draught
as if their wings were just brakes slowing the inevitable *splat*

What I want to say about pigeons
(whose same wings could be models for all those paintings of angels)

What I want to say is that their breasts are the exact
right size and shape to take an arrow

a delicate arrow from a child's bow,
head sharp as the point of a pencil.

Picture the pigeon high above the city.
The arrow zinging.

Picture them: arrow, pigeon,
the speed of their meeting,

the sudden end of flight.
Picture them falling:

Don't you want to paint that?
Pigeon and arrow falling?

Don't you?

First Word

O wallbirds, calendar birds, silent paper birds behind the open front door,
how you arrest my young daughter
each time we enter. Door shuts, her
mouth goes wide, a long ah,
for you as much as for the birds at the feeder:
fleet, elegant chickadees,
scrappy, hatchet-beaked finches,
darting juncos and flicks of bushtits.

You are none of you birds of myth—
not raven, crow, not dove, eagle—
you are nothing we have taken to ourselves
for ourselves. In your breasts beat
fast hearts. You are warmed
by feathers.

You are paper, you flesh.
You startle and fly,
you light, you roost.
You are not to be believed,
you are the first thing to fill
a one-year-old with wonder,
the first wish,
the first word:
bird.

Mouse

You saw it first   baked
I mean baked
on that rim below the broiler—
brittle grey bone-bag
splayed sidelong
puny-clawed stiff-tailed—
shocking you back
hand on your chest
oh god, yesterday's
remember?
banana bread
                oh god

Later you wanted to know
what would scare me like that
and I haven't found it, though
once on an island where we stopped for lunch
I went to pee and found
a dead great blue heron &
thought I'd take some feathers
but they didn't pop out,
I had to tug, had to put my sandal on the great dead bird
& really pull
                then I
grinned down to your kayak
waving
    as if it were easy as compost
    as if this wasn't close enough.

It wasn't, though.
I was showing off —
unshocked, locked
in safe skin
safe ears.
Rational.
Favoured.
Culpable.
One pin tumbler away
from a roaring heart.

Filleted Bass

one side neatly steaked & still brain

kept it twitching & flapping

under my knife

        the final tippy-tip of its tail like a dog's

I chiselled the last scrap of flesh

from its bones &

        tossed it to the gulls

A Bird in the House

I heard a cheep. A bird outside, I thought, but no.
A bushtit had flown in the open window.

You know what followed: wings' mad flap at glass
that looks like air, a light persistent bash

against what kept it there. I tried to guide it with
my hand. It wouldn't go. It thought it knew the path

and whapped the same sad barrier. My heart rate sped.
I'd have to catch it, all that frantic wildness fed

by fear. But in my two-hand cage its ounce was light
as air itself, as what inspirits us: it might

revive the dead. I lifted it then let it go,
a second's work. I thought time might have slowed

or nature changed itself, the bird thankful or tamed.
Bird stayed bird: wingbeat tree wind rain.

Crows Have Funerals, Did You Know That?

Crows only lie when dead, like this one
black on next door's green,
flight gear folded, bead eyes shut.
Petite technicians crouch next it,
gather data with sticks:
no blood, no pellet-nick, neck
intact. Natural causes? Age?
Mercury poisoning, lead?

Afternoon a flock of them paddles up street —
sixty, seventy birds whop-whopping air —
eddy out in nearest horse chestnut,
coughing, feathering there by what — friend?
Cousin? Ur-kin? Or just erst-crow? How do they know?
But they do. Where to come, anyway, and who knows?
What to say, too. How to hang back, sermonless,
loose and raucous. Unlike

my sister and me at the funeral home
(whose door till then we'd heaved just
to yell *how's life* down dim halls)
trussed in stiff dresses, warned off
the next room with its stiff tenant:
great-aunt in satiny half-open box,
churchy relatives filing by.

Our brothers looked, not me. I wanted to
but feared I'd be said morbid or curious,
knew I was there to be decorous, sad.
Failing one, I played up the other,

wondering what it was all for, murmurs
and nothings cooed across handshakes,
dry kisses, cousins catching up.
In the car we debated how ours'd be.
Not like this. That's all we knew.
Here the crows are loud, concupiscent,
tree-bound as long as they can handle —
a few minutes? three?
calling   Aw
            Aw

Rapala

wounded minnow, puppet,
i furrow water with invisible spade

bars on belly
like light in water

my eye sees your eye
i'm a mimic, i'm amphibian

out of water
i'm a fish

in water some-
thing else

an idea, a hook
allure

Every day the crows chase the eagles

Hello, coyote. Did you eat my neighbour's cat?
He's missing. The crow in the poplars
ate our baby finch. What do you mean it wasn't ours?
It fledged on our back porch.
We stood on a chair and peeked out the bathroom window.
We saw its yawping mouth. Beneath
the eagle's nest are black feathers, goose femurs, mallard down,
breastbones like sails,
birders.

Thug

What I remember doesn't matter anymore and
and probably never did
though it seemed to
(Though is a thug)

Wasps crawl in everywhere and
it is not just us
all the neighbours have them and
and rats, too.

I saw an eagle carry a rat last week.
Crows flew after it.
I thought the rat-tail was a shoelace. Why
is that eagle carrying a —
                              Oh.
In the up and down of the wingbeats
the heavy little rope of a tail
danced.

Dutch Elm Disease, 6th Line

Six snowy elms pitch against wind,
rot, fever.

After a time: whomp.

     Whole limbs drop to snow,
subside beneath it.

     Woodblock bop bop bop of beak.
     Wind.

        Snow snakes.

Whomp.

Glory trees
dying like empire

          of empire's disease.

Photo, Main Street Antique Shop

foursquare women locked in place by twenty year struts
solid as the barn that must be out back

their eyes look four different ways like
they'd had plans and then daughters

the oldest, silver hair combed flat, frowns
        eyes the weather   never admitted to plans:
hard bright jewels that wad together in her pocket now
like candies gone through the wash

the next, grand in soft ruffled shirt-front, pinned-up hair, dark pebble eyes
knows hers the romance everyone talked about, talks
about still don't they talk about it who's
that on the road, are they coming in?

the next, practical, impatient, her arms
yearning to lift to carry to not be still this is how she forgets
this is how she remembers who
she is the lilacs need pruning

the youngest rolls saliva around her eager mouth
looks straight at the
camera

The Birds Fall Down

I read a description of woodcocks rising in a wood
by a made-up man to his made-up granddaughter.
He was Russian and nostalgic and wanted her to know
how beautiful these birds he'd moments later shoot.

Somewhere are there photos of woodcock shoots,
Russian woodcock shoots in eighteen-ninety?
Somewhere there may be. Somewhere there may.
But in seventeen-ninety, no. Then, no photos,

no snick of shutter, no trap of light on salts,
no instant memory. Are there then
paintings of woodcocks flushed in early morning,
Russian woodcocks flushed in seventeen-ninety?

Somewhere there may be. Somewhere there may.
And any other year some picture, some drawing,
some charcoal on wall could try the same thing as
fictional aristocrat longing in exile for the beautiful

birds of his youth, about to be shot, but not shot, not yet.
And before that, long before, before steel, before guns,
before Russia, before fields, before writing, did some
grandfather watch woodcocks rising in his youth

and want in old age to tell his granddaughter how beautiful?
What does it say if we think no or yes? If yes,
there must have been, a man, at least one, who so loved
woodcocks he wanted to tell someone else how beautiful,

what does it say about us? The urge to art is what I'm getting at.
Experience more banal than art makes it we record
all day long, spider's-eye views of bank
line-ups, birthday cakes, the baby's ah-ah.

Somewhere now is a man with a microphone mid-
parabola aiming his sound gun at flushing birds.
Somewhere videographer, camera on stick-end,
clocks aardvark, mongoose, raccoon, viper.

All over now are people mechanically spooling
and unspooling reels of listening, capturing ribbon:
The Smithsonian's Sounds of the Office, 1964,
your vacationing neighbour's day at the seashore.

Before this, before, grandfather could tell granddaughter
and no one would know unless granddaughter told son
or sister or grandson. And that would be the end of it.

How many have read the passage I've read?
I've no way of knowing. Five thousand? Ten? Less? More?
All of us knowing, for a moment at least, how
on a cold Russian morning woodcocks fly up to be shot.

Before art there is no before, or there always is.
The archivist's vaults fill and fill.

Ben's Fall

For the sake of the story I pretend I was there shaking the flimsy bridge
behind Mr. Molson's turned back, fabricating my guilt — it's a story
after all, my story of Ben's fall. But I missed the good part — wet shoes
on a rope bridge, twelve-year-old tall as he'll ever be, six feet, falling his
own height into the Boyne river. His white-eyed silent shock before his
screams crash through still air, the rolling waves of his pain washing up
the valley turning back on themselves like the stream carrying his blood
roiling up against the beaver dam, settling in a backwater pool where one
lone leech undulates in a frenzy, the suspended blood its inkling of god.

Cindy's Fall

A year later we meet at a party, this woman, sent so easily off
a cliff by one small stone on the trail, and I, who went after
her, finding one ski, then the other, then poles,
gloves, glasses, blood on the snow, and finally her,
clasped in the V of two fallen trees, and just coming to.

Do we share a bond? a smiling man at the party wants to know,
and like liars on a sit-com
we might have sputtered *No-yes . . . yes-no*, truth
not being the issue here but comfort,
and why should we tell him, anyway?

You were so polite, I say to her instead. *You kept asking my name
and saying, "Thank you, Anne. Thank you for being here," as if
you were at a cocktail party,* which we are, now, and it's clear
she doesn't want to hear the whole story, how she looped
every half-minute and like a brained cartoon character
could not remember where she was, how she got
there, or who on earth I might be.

She wants to know even less how tautly her name, same as my beloved,
rose from my throat as my mind dug in with my boot-to-boot drop
to the place I would find her broken or dead. How her face
hung before me all that night — her marble-round eyes,
her blood-locked hair — all that night, the night my love
slept by another's side. Her face, her eyes, her hair,
her shocked unmasked voice: *Thank you, Anne.*
Thank you for being here.

Birds

Finches feed at the feeder.
Sparrows spruce up the cedar.
Chickadees zip through the laurel.
Hermit thrush hide under sorel.
Owls prowl in the oak.
Magpies crack a good joke.
Starlings line the pines.
Mourning doves pine on the lines.
Crows mourn their dead.
Seagulls unload on your head.

Sea gulls dog fish truck down Clark

Sea gulls dog fish truck down Clark,
coast even with truck's square butt,
light at red light, loft at green,
float paint-white dock-grey on diesel-blue air.

Lookit them dicker and
dive up there, engineless,
chasing what we've scooped from the sea,
locked away in a bin.

Walking & Falling

i.
say you are a raccoon
and you are walking along a fence
and your bulk teeters
and falls

iii.
say you are eighty-six
and there's a dead raccoon on the spike you used to prop up your fence
and you try to lift it off with a shovel
but it's stuck, plus your arm doesn't lift above the shoulder

v.
just say, for instance, you are that raccoon
walking along that fence

say you are that kid
lying asleep at night

that raccoon-lifter
unconscious at the bottom of the stairs

ii.
say you are a kid
and your ball goes under the skirt of the spruce
and you go to get the ball
but it's beside a dead raccoon

iv.
say the yard is square
say life is long
and always ends in tragedy
no wait, comedy

autobiography

Disappointment

That can of paint in the shed since we moved in, turns out
it's oil paint, wh^{ch} I discovered only
when the stairs were done &
I went to rinse out brush wh^{ch} of course would
n't rinse. My hands are all
white. There's nothing to clean my hands.
The paint'll take a while to dry.
Sorry.

I didn't get that job I wanted, the one I took this job in hopes of getting.
It's not fair but what is?
You, I guess.
     Rain.
The earth turning. Chemical
reactions.

The dog has yeast in her ears.
No one knows how eels reproduce.
You can't use the stairs.

Bikes

First a green embarrassment (I should have been
stronger): triangle seat, skirt bar, flowered
white basket, one
speed.
        Holy, look at those muscles, Pete said to Jon
when he thought I couldn't hear (it wasn't a compliment).
I hauled on handlebars but I should have been
stronger.

Then Ian's yellow three-speed for twenty-five bucks:
booting down the dirt hill off the Yonge side of Strathgowan
into the ravine, the front wheel released itself, hooped a comic course
over rutted hardpack, at least at the time forks pronged dirt
I thought it was funny though now I can't remember why.
I wasn't hurt.

Some other ten-speed in here I forget because of
(flashing lights around this, please)
the Peugeot

God's bike
                no actually
just my brother's, too,
but God, that bike

.

I flew.
My thighs grew hard.
The leather saddle
cradled.

Ian came back, reclaimed his steed, and I bought
a crappy 12-speed I left four years later one pedal missing
in the garage of the house on Dovercourt
where I lived with the geniuses. It was the mountain
bike by then. Norco. Beat
all the cars in Toronto with it.
                                    In Kitchener, I let it
overwinter in the driveway, bought a car, grew careless,
watched the seat rot, did nothing until I bought a new seat,
packed up for Vancouver, locked the bike to another porch,
a year, two. Renewed acquaintance, set it up with new
slicks and the tenth ave bike route,
till hauling on the handlebars up Yukon away from work,
hauling just like on the girl's bike, Lawrence Crescent, age ten,
hauling just like up Keele, last big hill to my first big job,
something snapped.
The derailleur. Snapped
right off.

That's the last bike that mattered
though I've got a new one now,
had it ten years.
I ride it, it's not like it sits,
it's just not mythic.

Nothing is.

Hair

*"I had my hair washed to-night. We had a lovely wood
fire to dry it that crackled and sparked most beautifully."*
     —Patsy Murdoch, Saturday, September 11, 1943

In my mother's day, if your hair
was thick and long like hers,
washing it was an evening's work. It took hours
to dry. They lay in front of the fire,
hair out on towels. They roasted
chestnuts, popped corn, toasted
bread on long forks. Retired,
happy and warm to cold bedrooms,
fell into sleep and war dreams.

Our hair was done infrequently, too.
Our Dad, in one of two domestic tasks,
Scirocco'd it with a cloth-corded dryer. We'd ask
him to direct its cone of wind into
our open towels and he'd oblige, briefly,
then fluff our thin hair and pare our nails,
push back cuticles with his clean surgeon nails.
We'd hide winces, we'd say good-night stiffly.
In between washes, my hair grew greasy.
My mom pushed pigtails: "They're so easy!"

I pulled them out past view of the house
and went down to the park where stranger kids
asked, "Are you a boy or a girl?" I said
"girl" as a rule, sensing they'd browse
my crotch and find something lacking,
which they did that one time I was wearing
my red jeans and the boy was staring

right there at flatness. (It was years before I'd hear of packing.)
At the hairdresser, Mom said, "Just a trim.
Not too short. Make it feminine."

To me she said, "Why do you want to look
like a boy?" I said, "I don't." She said, "You do."
I said, "I want to look like me." It was true,
but she didn't buy it the thirty years or so it took
to come to some kind of truce, when she had it out
in a letter and promised to say nothing more.
In the meantime, she controlled what I wore:
girls' clothes: blouses, girls' jeans. I had zero clout.
I want not to blame her for all those years
of needless strife. But I do. It doesn't matter what I wear.

At twelve, with shoulder-length centre-part hair,
I went to a hairdresser south of Bloor on Yonge,
a cool one (it was advertised on CHUM).
My breasts were new: wee nipple-cones there
under my favourite blue and green striped T.
"Wow, you've got long hair for a boy," she said,
then thought the tears in my eyes were for losing said
hair, when they were all anxiety
about the nipples — would she spy them?
Spot me for a fraud? (Didn't know then that if she did, she'd deny them.)

Earlier that year, at music camp, at a snowball dance —
you know, where one pair starts,
then the DJ calls *Snowball* and the couple parts
and grabs from the sidelines some chance
new date — a girl took my hand,
tried to drag me onto the floor,

took my holding back for shyness and liked me more
but there were people who knew me and what if she found
out it wasn't a cute boy she was after
but an ugly girl? There'd be laughter

or worse. Wasn't the first time — train porters, other
girls at other dances, bus drivers, cops,
random grownups, people in shops —
wouldn't be the last. My poor mother
winced and corrected: no, my *daughter*
(later, two bank tellers: "Anne. That's a funny name
for a boy." "Isn't that usually a girl's name?")
tried to teach me what life had taught her.
"I feel nice and comfortable when I know I look nice,"
she wrote at thirteen. Not bad advice,

but I feel nice and comfortable when I know
I look comfortable. When I know I look like
a dyke
or a fag (men shout it out car windows
late at night, drunk). Like a schoolboy (British),
like some backwoods hack, like a Mod,
like a hoser, like a jock, like a Dad.
Anything else, sir? I enter washrooms, skittish,
head down, cued for the double-take: me, the skirted sign,
me, the shake of the head, the hard line,
You're in the wrong washroom, guy.
Am I?

God Save Miss Cressman

under her square brow her eyes like storm-chaser's storms
under her square jaw her don't-try-it chin

from her square shoulders her boxy cardigan
over her square hips her oblong skirt

on the right blackboard Robert Frost stopping in woods
under the morning's Lord's Prayer her rocking Wallabees

solomon of southern Ontario
grade five's great bird

may we defend her laws
and ever give her cause

to make the most of us   .
god's sorry kids

Reasons to Move Back to Ontario

Three Guelph century homes
for the price of one dank Vancouver bungalow.

The stone those houses are made of.
The quarry the stone's from.

Every back road's gravel pit.
Birches.

Roads laid out in a one-mile grid.
The words "concession road," "side road."

Airport Road, Brown's Line, QEW.
Poplar Side Road, Simcoe Road 10, Nottawasaga Side Road.

The names of townships: Gwillimbury, Mono,
East Garafraxa, Dumfries, Adjala.

The look of the dirt on dirt roads:
horse-brown on a cool wet day, ash on a hot.

The speed you can go over washboard in a pickup,
how much fishtail's good for a little fun, how much'll put you in the ditch.

Lakes that get warm in summer.
Small-mouth bass. Needle-nose gar.

The smell of granite and pine.
Highway sixty-nine.

Doughnuts within walking distance.
Outdoor skating rinks. Shinny.

The GO train. The TTC. The drive to Acton.
Stratford. Blyth. Toronto Island.

The smell of ravine dirt.
The smell of ravine water: copper, old poo.

My mother's childhood on the Humber.
My father's childhood on the Don.

Mine, in between.

Second-Hand Clothes

1

Bored of the flats, we create imaginary hills with our gaits, amateur
mimes in a group illusion. *Incline!* someone shouts, and we italicize
toward the next party, faces punching the February air. *Decline!* and
arms swing loose from backslashed bodies down the other side of the
flat trail. The joke without words, or laughter either, for that matter, until
Angela stops dead in her thigh-length twisted-braid old ladies' coat:
*What if the ghosts of the former owners of all my clothes came back to
haunt me?* A joke too, of course, but what if? What if?

2

Going up the t-bar, the ski patroller: *Bayonet wound?* What he's talking
about — it takes me a minute to figure out as I quit swinging my pole
into drifts, pulling up doughnuts of snow on the basket, and look at
him — is my army surplus wool pants with the vertical tear on the
inner thigh that is coming apart again, a new wound breaking away
from my clumsy stitches. *How's it feel to wear pants someone died
in?* The both of us laughing as if it couldn't be true, as if the pants he
died in must have been buried with him. If he was buried at all. If he
died. Maybe he was just wounded in these, H. Macdonald of the magic
marker on the inside pocket, and maybe he's alive today and marching
in Remembrance Day parades, misty-eyed and angry watching a
schoolboy his own long-gone age who trumpets the Last Post March
not knowing what it's like to grow out of a soldier's uniform.

3

In the echo of my mirrored jeans I'm someone else for a second, with
longer legs, a broader ass, heftier thighs and what's that there? Uh-oh,
the disquieting rub of testicles. He must've worn them tight — tighter
than me, but then I can almost take them off without undoing
them — to get that hint I've never noticed before, that faint fade mark
either side of the seam below the fly.

My sudden secret: I want to keep them for a moment, the balls the
mirror's given me, to know the weight and bulk of flesh between my
legs, the fragility of exposed genitals, the powered daring of simply
sitting, legs apart.

.

Back Roads, Clouds

Driving home from Orangeville after a hockey tournament,
sweat dry on our skin, wet gear in the back like sleeping dogs,
stereo loud, we drive on cloud
wispy as blown snow.
It holds us aloft the whole way home.

Years passed this way: the two of us driving back roads
on clouds to and from small towns.

Years passed. The clouds held us aloft
and then let us down.

Skate

In winter afternoons we strap on skates
and guide our clumsy kitchen chairs cross scarred
and snowy ice. Behind our parents' eyes
appears a pinhole memory of grace,
and leaving us to scrabble rink's round yard,
they're off for once alone. Four blades surprise
their sleeping feet awake, grey sleeves lift green
and living limbs round shoulder, waist.
Their breasts iridesce, coattails scissor,
they zoom and swoop, summer bright, keen
precisionists of flight, of veer, they brace
and turn, they spin and spear, forget their lesser
selves. Our parents skate away from us
to joy, and then skate back as if they must.

Address

This is my dad, happy
        in a canoe
            long legs tossed out before him
    arms paddling like legs walk

This is my dad
        fedora floppy
            balsam sprig pinned to nose by glasses
                so every breath's a wilderness

            On portages, he made balsam boats
poked a pocket of sap with a snapped twig
        found a quiet pool to drop it in
                    the rainbow bloom like gas on the dark water
    the chemistry lesson, propulsion
Off they would go
        little adventurers
    on joy-rides
        the middle of
            no
                where

Once, in his youth, a letter reached him at this address:
    Ross
        Algonquin Park
            Ontario

Thief

There it was at the beach
  its writhes
its sculling hands
  its syncopated surges:
my mother's walk.

The walk was in
  the body of someone else
holding the hand of a man
  like my dad

younger stouter
  but with the same swing of happiness
or optimism. *I am walking with my wife.*
  What's the problem?

Now I am trying to picture her old walk
  before Parkinson's torqued it
but it's so long ago
  and so ordinary

I can barely make it out.
  The walk elides her, this woman
I don't know. The woman I did know
  is gone.

Unemployment

They could be other places,
in Business with the Dow-Jones
or by the racing results in Sports,
but maybe the editors figure
gamblers are too far gone
to take heart in the stars
and in any case
don't want the competition.

And really,
who needs them more
than us pawers of want ads?
The balm of their type
after pages of squint,
the bob of their lock
in canals of print,

the jaunty horoscopes
pearling the swine
with promise of lucre
a savvy hunch brings dollars
friends loyal, lovers true
a friend brings a career boost
expect ecstasy after dark
old advice good as new
be patient
don't spend or lend
a big breakfast gets you off to a good start

Our ambition is strong.
Our lucky stars are shining.
We could sing from pleasure.

Notes to self re: world water day poem

—put in something on the history of fountains
—something on chemistry, how hard it is to fathom atoms,
       protons, neutrons, let alone compounds, valencies, two
       hydrogen and one oxygen
—something about drinking two hydrogen one oxygen
       six beer
—something on eyeballs, how they dry out
—something on eyeball first aid: dixie cups, tape
—something on saliva
—something on thirst
—something on the average volume of the average toilet tank
       & that time the pipes burst at that cottage I rented &
       I filled the tank with Nalgene bottles of spring run-off
—something about gravity
—something about tides
       swells, the Dead Sea, the Great Lakes, the
       Aral Sea all dust now
—something on heavy metals in the lungs
—something about coffee
—something about decaffination
—something on bottled water
       the Coca-Cola company, how I don't ever want to pay them for
       water in my life
—something on taps—
       actually a lot on taps:
       on/off on/off on/off on/off on/off
       and other things too like kinds of taps, spiggots, self-closing taps
       timers for taps, taps the song (dunh da-nuh/dunh-na-na), taps
       for water
—something on giardia, or no, cholera
—something on rust
—something on babies

—something on the movie "Chinatown"
—something on the 3 Gorges dam, the Grand Coulee dam
        the Revelstoke dam
—something about kokanee
—more on the Aral Sea
—something on sloughs
—something on tarns
—something on oxbows
—something on Smetana's the Moldau
—something on fens, bogs, marshes, swamps
—something on ducks
—something on the water table, maybe
—something on waterbeds
—something on gutters
—something on ice
—something on how when we were thirsty we used to tip
        our paddles up and drink from them, put our lips
        next to the blade and let lakewater run into our mouths
—something on how sweet it was, Ontario lakewater, like
        maple sap dripping from spiggots, just exactly
        that sweet

Winter at the Outdoor Ed Centre

Half of the people who worked at the outdoor ed centre knit. The men who knit knitted hats and scarves. The women all knit. One was trying an Icelandic sweater and another socks. The road was too long to plough. They brought everything in on snowmobiles. During the day they took children on snowshoe hikes and taught them how to make shelters out of densely packed piles of snow. In the evenings they took the children on nighttime snowshoe hikes and indoors taught them face-pulling games and cat's cradle. Then they took the children out into winter's night and bounced them one by one high into the air from a large round blanket. The children begged to stay on longer and be tossed higher. The stars made the galaxy deep. After that the children had a snack and their teachers put them to bed and the people who worked at the outdoor ed centre sat by the fire with their feet up and knit. Two of the women were lovers. One of the men loved one of the women hopelessly. The woman knitting a sweater whose lover was in Toronto becoming lovers with other people left no room for the arm holes and had to unravel the entire yoke of the nearly finished sweater.

Spring

Breakup.
The sap ran. We tapped
it. No kids that week. Varnished gunwhales. Ran
into town. There was a beer strike.
We'd forgot.

It was the age of VCR rentals. You
could rent a TV too. It was the age of
Canada Coolers.

Back of Home Hardware
on the tin lid under a film of dust
Miss Varethane posed, all short shorts, all
roller skates, all lift and
separate.
                              We'd forgot about the beer strike.

That's how I ended up
back of the snowmobile, TV
on lap, pack full of VCR and videos and Miss
Varethane. It was the age of Canada Coolers. They clanked in the pack.
Jeff gunned it up the hill.
I fell off the back.

Snow melted.
We counted the number of times Tony Montana said fuck.
We watched the bodies fall.
Jason ran through the woods in his mask.
Jeff stood beside the TV, watched me watch bodies fall.

We were alone. It was the off-season. The lake ice
rarely groaned. The tree
we tapped whose sap
never ran was
an oak.

Compliments/Insults

You run like a boy.
You skate like a boy.
You [climb]
    [ski]
    [hurdle]
    [smoke]
    [swear]
    [vandalize]
    [etc.] like a boy.
You're strong.
You have big shoulders.
You don't play trombone like a girl at all.
I don't know any other girls who listen to Rick Wakeman.
You're pretty good at math.
You're pretty funny.
You're not like most girls I know.
I've never met anyone like you.
I can't imagine you in a skirt.
You throw like a girl.

Anniversary

I'd like to give you a long slow drink of water
a thirst

I'd like to give you a full set of teeth
something to bite

a straw
something to suck on
a long slow drink of water

a field
grain
pebbles
earth

I'd like to give you an edge of sand
a lip a tongue a cornered snail
a long slow drink of water

I'd like to give you a hole in the ground
a step a mouth a flight
a blue night
a blink
a long slow drink
a long slow drink of water

Questions for Isabelle Gunn

who joined the Hudson's Bay Company
as John Fubister, 1806

Was it love

Was it love made you follow
the young men out of Orkney
to Hudson's Bay mornings
where a night's worth of breath
caulked gap-ridden walls
with 6 inches of ice?

Was it love swung your legs
in that sure rough-ground trot?
the gunwhale-laden slog through
bog and bush and back
blackfly conventions
lacing your neck

You could have had it all at home
the ice and the work
tho maybe not the blackflies

So I want to know, Isabelle Gunn

Love or £6, or
something else again?

Did you rip

When weeks of cloud took the moon
when days got lost in the river
and blood began between one stroke and the next

Gadzooks, I gotta shit again lads
hold on

Did you rip your longjohns
stiff already with sweat
and more running down your face
more still between the small breasts
on your large body

Sweat and breasts
and stiff wads chafing

⅄

Was the price

Did he want you as a man or
did he catch you squatting to pee

Was the price of his silence
a fuck in the woods

A nod of his head
a punch on your too-soft chest

Eh, mate. Eh, John.
Did he rest his head

on your breasts
when he found them?

Did you wreak

You had to know the game was almost up
when the blood stayed in your womb for once
but never having heard of Pope Joan
maybe you thought you'd proven yourself

How much did you eat to mask the mound with flesh?
How stout did you grow with the months and miles
between Albany and Pembina, and how strong
before you asked to lie down in an officer's house?

Three days after Christmas did you think about death
calling out to the man who would write your life
in his journal that night, drunk and prone to exaggeration
at the best of times, his own wife softly home in England?

"Death before washtubs," is what I hear you say
even in the throes of your son's (your son's!) birth
instead of his mimicky high-pitched lie: "Oh please sir,
be kind to a poor, helpless, abandoned wretch."

Did you wreak your revenge with poorly washed clothes?
Tobacco-chewing hag sending horks into the washtub,
brewing trousers slick with unrinsed soap, chortling,
as the factor scratches his raw starchy neck

and prays on his knees for the next boat out.

Did you forfeit

They didn't all come home, the young men
who set out with fairy tale futures.
Five years in the bush'll do that to a man,
spoil him for the slow route of the plough
along furrow after furrow in a finite land.

You too were "not inclined to come home"
even back at Albany, in skirts, under eyes.
But you didn't have a choice, no chance
to jump ship with your squalling infant
to love the bush that Susanna roughed.

Did you forfeit your pay along with your freedom?
Poverty and propriety hand in hand again,
your world shrinking to the size of your room,
to the knitting needles, to the spindle, to the yarn,
the baby growing hard, up to his father's height.

Three years in the bush, fifty-two back in Orkney.
Sure you must have been bored and mad,
enough to enjoy the fleeing children's squeals
as you walked their streets, delivered their stockings,
the sting of their skipping song lashing your ear.

Isabelle Gunn, Isabelle Gunn,
couldn't get a man so she made herself one.
Isabelle Gunn, Isabelle Gunn,
left as a man, came back with a son.

You died alone, four men's entries marking your life,
captain, trader, schoolteacher, inspector of the poor,
ballads, legends and history squeezed from their words.
I have the good grace to ask questions;
         you have no tongue to set me right.

Bright darkness: the poetry of Lord Byron presented in the context of his life & times

if you stacked all the norton anthologies in the world
and made a house of them
it would burn easily
but it would burn bright
and it might be a skyscraper
so you'd need rebar
spearing the great authors
speaking of which (spearing)
I don't advocate the burning of books
but if you roasted the norton anthology on a stick
wouldn't the pages flail open
the book going cylindrical like books do in the rain
where the spine curves into the core and
pages radiate like sea star arms
or anemones?
so maybe first what you do is you soak the norton
anthology great authors edition and then you
let it fan out to dry
and then you put it on a stick and hold it over the coals
and then it goes that slow slow fast way that
things catch fire
the flames all golden
and bright
in the
darkness
and Lord Byron cries out, "My life and times!"
and Beowulf howls
and Beckett's eyebrows crackle
and Lord Byron cries out, "My life and times!"
and the Faerie Queen pops, sparks,
and Milton mutters right along.

Found

In a 1950s-vintage
Madame Bovary, a small,
faded, turquoise-and-
white pamphlet:
> *Instruction in the use of Ramses*
> *Vaginal Jelly.*

In a lurid paperback *Jane Eyre,*
a HELLO MY NAME IS sticker
wobbly with newly learned cursive:
> *Dear Santa, I left these cookies for you. I made them my self. I hope*
> *you like them Love, Kevin*
> *p.s. Do you like the New Kids On the Block Yes or no*

In *The Curse of Doone*
(A Genuine Paperback Library Gothic)
not just this sentence— *He had never been attracted by convention*
> *in any shape or form —before his groggy knee and jobs of*
> *increasing importance on the Continent had forced him to give up*
> *the game, he had been the most unorthodox, if brilliant, Rugby*
> *three-quarter of his day —and, ridiculous as the feeling was, he*
> *felt relieved that this girl was not 'usual in appearance' —*

but the address
of a Dutch mouth organ club
in red ink

In *Benéts Readers Encyclopedia*, under Nihilism:
> a junk's sail of pressed blossom laid across *revolution*

Rule of the game

This interesting rod-lifting game
requires quiescence, skill and concen-
tration. Rods are taken in the hand so that
the fist will lie on the table. It is by
suddenly opening the hand that the rods
fall on to the table, describing
a circle. In case of an unsatisfactory
throw the player is allowed to repeat
that throw.

Now the player tries to lift the rods
individually with the fingers without
other rods however being allowed to
move. When the Mikado has been lifted,
it may be used for the lifting of fur-
ther rods.

It is by pressing the finger on the tip
of the rod that the rod may be lifted
most easily.

If another rod is moved then the number
of points won must be totalled up; the
next player may then begin with a new
throw. The number of rounds to be
played should be agreed upon before
play begins. The winner will be he
who has won the largest number of
points.

We wish you good entertainment!

June 21

It's
barely summer
and already the
long decline is on:
tomorrow, four seconds' light go.
Day after, say goodbye to fourteen.
Then it's 29, then 50, light parabolaing
away from us, darkness creeping up the graph.
By the time school's out and it's really summer,
we're already four odd minutes in the hole to winter.
So why "Midsummer"? Whose night? What dreams? I'm middle-aged. Peaches are hard
yellow balls you could bean someone with. They will soften, though (unless
the hail gets them, unless the bees fail). They'll drop. Peach juice will
run down chins. And that's the reason to light the fire, the bone fire,
to drink what's fermented (what decay has turned to spirit), to dance, forget the dead
this one short night when it seems like we don't have to die after all. Look
what we do with plain old angles, with the accident of geography: turn them into hope. See
how light it is? This will come back. But meanwhile let's throw light at what dark is left,
let's juggle it on sticks, let's spit it off our tongues, let's shoot it up into the air, kapow,
we can banish even night, doesn't our revelry say so? And if not, oh well. We had a good time.
Look, the sun's coming up. The world has spun again. How are you? We have so much to look forward to.

Butler Says

Butler says observe.
Butler says hail.
Butler says matter.
Butler says reject.
Butler says protest.
Butler says fulfill.
Butler says be.
Don't.

Butler says determine.
Butler says impersonate.
Butler says find.
Butler says see.
Butler says do.
Butler says opt.
Except.

Butler says formulate.
Butler says deny.
Butler says become.
Butler says constitute.
Butler says talk.
Call.
Say.

Butler says change.
Butler says have.
Butler says propose.
Butler says subvert.
Butler says disrupt.

Butler says give.
Butler says frame.
Butler says accord.
Butler says structure.

Exist.

Special publicity and enforcement of California's belt use law

Belts must be worn!
This is California.
There's a reason they put those loops on waistbands.
For belts!

Belts, Baby.

An empty belt loop is not only sad, it's illegal!
It's not only illegal, it's sad.
Sad, and illegal, Baby.

Babies Over 40

They're bald.
The boys. The girls' hair is just thinning.
They're always crying about this and that, you can't even tell *what*
    they're crying about. I'm hungry. I'm tired. I need
    a change.
Their driver's licenses have expired.
They fall asleep on long drives. It's the only way
    you can get them to sleep sometimes. At night they
    lie awake. Their sighs shake the bed.
They can't see anything closer than the end of their arms.
They have gas.
Don't shake them, no matter how mad you are. Walk away and count to ten.
What are they crying about? Who knows. It doesn't matter. Walk away and
    count the miles. One. Two. Three. Four. Miles are longer
    than kilometres. Six. Seven.
At home, they weep and lace their shoes. They run past you at mile
    nine, crying. They are training for a marathon. Their tears
    are not related.

New Frontiers in Conception

Well like yeah. I couldn't really
yeah
so like yeah like
I don't know
yeah
like I can never get past the
    yeah

yeah I was yeah
so I don't   .
yeah
yeah if only yeah
but yeah
no listen yeah yeah seriously
yeah
no but I mean yeah
yeah
no

Preliminary Results Using SOBSA for Non-Invasive Determination of Ulna Bending Stiffness

1. Ulnas bend.
2. But they're also stiff. Like skis.
3. Like if you put your knee to someone's forearm like it's a stick? And you pull with your hands while pushing with your knee? It won't snap right away. It'll bend first.
4. Sobs may result.
5. Don't snap it, though. That was just an example. Snapping the ulna would be invasive. We want non-invasive.

(1) Women and the (2) Spoils of Success

(1)	(2)
Donna.	Muffins.
Agnes.	BMXes.
Pat.	Cartographies.
Pat.	Rainforests.
Brittany.	Really nice pens.
Ndidi.	Pot-bellied pigs.
Ruth.	Waffle irons.
Maria.	Pencil skirts.
Marina.	Gym membership.
Maia.	Private bouts of massive doubt.
Leigh.	Executive assistant.
Mala.	Grief.
Nadia.	Wigs.
Simone.	Ulcers.
Sunni.	Sleeping pills.
Farrah.	Granite island.
Alessandra.	The farm. Several sunny meadows with horses in them.
Val.	Healthy gums.
Ninu.	Blue sky.
Choi Ping.	Hair extensions.
Rosmina.	Organic lemons.

Learning disabilities

Or, as they say, leaning diabetes
Or rather, yearly debates, er, early debuts
yubba dubba

du

The Highway Loss Data Institute

It is the saddest institute

nobody in it
but everyone heading there
thumbs out.

What gets lost on highways
is more than we knew we had.

Its fonds are the deepest fonds.

In Bella Coola that summer, we hitchhiked.
It's how you got to the pool on a July day.
The dusty backs of trucks.

It's how you do   or don't
get into   town   or   home   today   or to-
      morrow   or   the
  next or   any
                day

    if you live on highways (16 or 5 or 97 or)
      where
        the Indian Act has
      slapped you

the highway loss data institute is
weeping from its cinder blocks, its tar-and-pebble roof

around it the water rises.
When it subsides again let's say power has shifted

let's say power has shifted now
and we are free to right wrongs

there's no water
there's no institute

we are free to right wrongs

Relaxation for Concentration, Stress Management and Pain Control Using the Fleming Method

Lie on your back
like a frog with a finger to its chest.
Kick your legs.
Kick again.
Kick quite a lot.
Now give up.
Feel your skin,
thinner than paper, thinner than
the film between layers of onion grade fives put under microscopes.
Feel the skin under the finger wrinkle.
Feel the lead in the air seeping in.
Kick. Kick half-heartedly.
Lie back, all muscle and skin.
Lie back.
Croak.

13 ways of looking at a pair of underpants

I

With eyes through the leg holes,
naturally. (What part you drape over
the nose is up to you.)

II

A-soak in the sink.
I was bare-butted in my jeans,
out of pairs.

III

The underpants whipped in the autumn winds.
It was a small part of the pantomime.

IV

A man and a woman can wear the
same pair.
A man and a woman and underpants
are one.

V

Stacked in a drawer,
all the waistbands lined up
in darkness.

VI

In flight from hand to floor,
I do not know which to prefer,
the beauty of the faint whump as they light
or just after.

VII

O thin men of Saanich,
why do you imagine golden underpants?
Do you not see how the black gotch
slips off the foot of the women about you?

VIII

The underpants know nothing.
There is nothing the underpants know.

IX

The underpants understand the underbody
under the undertaker.

X

Twirling around a finger.
Zing, zing, zing.

XI

The shadow on the grass
of underpants that hang on the line
quavers and can't be worn.

XII

The toilet is flushing.
The underpants must be pulled up.

XIII

It was evening all afternoon.
My underpants were creeping
and were going to creep.
They wept in the wet dawn.

Notes

"Butler Says" was written by googling "Judith Butler says" and then taking the first verb after the phrase in the results and putting it in the imperative. The variant lines were found by googling "Butler doesn't say" and taking the next verb.

The academia.edu series ("Special Publicity...," "New Frontiers in Conception," "Preliminary Results...," "Women and the Spoils of Success," "Babies over 40," "...the Fleming Method," "Learning Disabilities," "The Highway Loss Data Institute," "Bright darkness: the poetry of Lord Byron...") were composed using titles of articles that the site academia.edu thought might be written by me.

"June 21" was written for the CBC Radio feature A Verse to Summer, wherein listeners suggest summery subjects for poems and Jake Kennedy imposes a constraint. In this case, the listener suggested summer solstice and Jake decreed a poem that was 21 lines long with the first line one word, the second line two words, the third line three, and so on.

"Rule of the game" is a transcription of the English language instructional insert for the game Mikado Spiel, a version of Pick-up Sticks.

"13 Ways of Looking at a Pair of Underpants" is, I hope needless to say, a rip-off of Wallace Stevens's "Thirteen Ways of Looking at a Blackbird."

Acknowledgements

Big thanks to Beth Follett, and to Cindy Holmes, Jake Kennedy, Leslie Walker Williams, and Michael V. Smith, who liked the chapbook enough to imagine a book book and gave me their readerly eyes and their enthusiasm. Susan Holbrook, too, and Tannis Nielsen: thank you. Thanks also to Shannon Stewart all those years ago, and to Jon Pearce for *Mirrors*, 1975.

"Questions for Isabelle Gunn" originally appeared in *Prairie Fire* and "Second-Hand Clothes" in *Fiddlehead*.

Anne Fleming is the author of *Gay Dwarves of America*, a finalist for the Ethel Wilson Fiction Prize, the novel, *Anomaly*, and *Pool-Hopping and Other Stories*, shortlisted for a BC Book Prize and the Governor-General's award. She grew up in Toronto and now divides her time between Vancouver and Kelowna.